Why Love is Important, Even if at Times Painful

CHAPTER 0 from the
'Find Love or Die Trying' Series.

Christopher Conway

YOUR FREE GIFT

Finding Your Soulmate Tips Sheet

Sometimes you need a quick tip for a situation. This tips sheet points you to the best resources to help you fast!
(Get Yours Now...It's FREE)

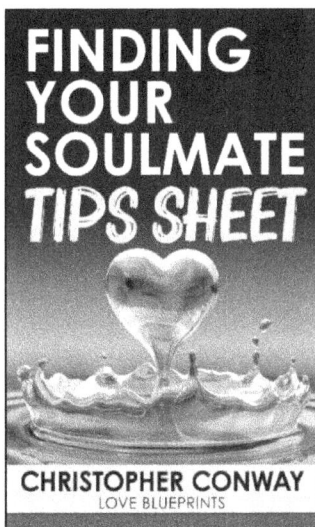

Request FREE Tips Sheet Today. Go to:
https://loveblueprints.com/fldt-tips-sheet/

PROLOGUE

In your grasp, you have Chapter 0 from the *Find Love or Die Trying* series created by Christopher Conway of LoveBlueprints.com. The series' mission is to provide lovers of love the power to find, manage and enjoy love.

The chapters in the *Find Love or Die Trying* series provide answers to the most complicated love questions you go to bed confused about each night.

Does the thought of love scare you? You get the out-of-control feeling where your partner has you in their grasp. What exactly is love, and why does it make you feel so possessed?

Love is not a game. Love can save or destroy you. But love is a basic human need that you must have to feel human.

To avoid depression, anxiety, and loneliness, you need a balance between giving and receiving love, even if it's painful at times.

What To Expect from Chapter 0

In Chapter 0, '**Why Love is Important, Even if at Times Painful,**' Mr. Conway reveals what most books fail to tell about why romantic love necessary.

And it's just only about sex. You don't need sex to

have love or vice-versa.

Inside this chapter, you learn how love as a child affects your ability to love or receive love as an adult. If you want to find your soulmate one day, you must understand why love is essential, even if at times painful.

Unlike most books which are thin love stories about how one person found Love, Christopher Conway outlines a common-sense explanation into how your view of love might be hurting your ability to find someone to love you.

Why Love is the One Drug Your Body Needs

Love is more profound than romance. Giving and receiving love are equally important. When you are "pent" up with love, you need to channel it somewhere. This is why you need a soulmate.

Maya Angelou, American poet, actress, and credited with a list of plays, movies, and television shows spanning over 50 years, once said:

Love is like a virus. It can happen to anybody at any time."

You have no control of love when it hits you. What you can do is be prepared when it hits. In Chapter 0, **'Why Love is Important, Even If at Times Painful,'**

Mr. Conway covers:

- Why love must be part of your world if you want happiness

- How the absence of love in your life can make you crazy

- Why love has to be painful at times, but still worth the fight

- What are the signs that accompany romantic love

- What happens when you do not experience love in your life

Mr. Conway's Promise to You

After you go through Chapter 0 and fully absorb why love is essential, you will have the courage to open your heart to its power and goodness. Once this happens, your soulmate is sure to follow next.

Without the knowledge in this chapter, love may never find you because you will not understand why the pain of love is at times necessary to enjoy its sweetness. It can be a cold, bitter, lonely world without love.

The time is now to seize the benefits of romantic love. The longer you wait, the colder and harder your heart becomes.

It becomes so cold that love can never find its way

inside. At that point, life may not be worth it anymore.

This is why you need to use the strategies in Chapter 0, **'*Why Love is Important, Even if at Times Painful,*'** by Christopher Conway today.

Let's dive into Chapter 0 right now!

CHAPTER 0: WHY LOVE IS IMPORTANT, EVEN IF AT TIMES PAINFUL

…and why you must have it to survive!.

One of the most tremendous forces of the universe is the power of love; a supernatural power that can grab hold of anything and anyone and cause noticeable changes almost immediately. Everyone seeks love in their life. It could be the love of a mother desired by a child or the father's attention sought by a teenager.

It could also be the trust of a business partner as a responsible person or the attention and care of a romantic partner.

In any case, all these are expressions of love that people crave in their lives. Usually, the quality of life a person will live (when all the chips are down) depends on the quality of love, care, and attention they receive from the people who matter to them.

When people do not get the requisite level of love they need at the right time, there is every tendency that they may deteriorate or begin to experience the need to release their hurts and frustrations in several different ways.

Love and the presence or absence of it in a person's life

This is why much of the research and observations that have been carried out reveal that children who did not get the necessary amount of love and care from their parents when they were children often treat their children the same way they were treated.

Some of them go on to become monsters in their homes. They might even resort to societal vices that keep everyone in contact with them on their toes, and in a bad way.

All these can be traced down to one thing; love and the presence or absence of it in a person's life. This raises a few questions in the mind of every logical person. What is love?

What is this mysterious and powerful force that shapes or at least affect how people interact with themselves and the world at large?

Why is this love so important? Is there any way

to remedy the absence of love in a person's life? Why should the lack of love pose such a threat to a person? This chapter will examine all these concepts quickly and look at what makes 'love' so important and influential in people's lives.

Let's start at the beginning.

What is "love?"

This is arguably one of the most challenging questions anyone can ask in today's world. This is because there are many resources available on the subject matter, and all these offer their suggestions on what love is and the classical ways love can be expressed.

To have a better grip of what love truly is, let us take a quick look at the definitions available to the public.

According to Wikipedia, love encompasses a range of robust and positive emotional and mental states. Most of which can be attributed to a sublime virtue or good habits, the deepest interpersonal affections, or the simplest pleasures.

Some other sources define love as a state of mind or a force that creates a feeling of fondness, contentment, and happiness in the mind and heart of a person who feels it for someone else.

What this implies is that when a person loves

another, they are positively disposed toward them. They begin to act, talk, and respond to the person in a completely different way.

At times, they place the person's happiness above theirs and would do anything to make sure that the person they love feels safe and cherished when they are with them.

A study carried out revealed that love is everywhere (or almost everywhere). This study examined 166 worldwide cultures (even those that were considered to be archaic and barbaric).

This study revealed that out of the 166 cultures closely observed, love was present in 147. These cultures had unique ways of expressing love, but the deep-seated feelings remained fond of fondness, admiration, and trust.

When love is used in a romantic context, the expression used to describe it is usually the term "in-love." This implies that the people being talked about enjoy a kind of romantic inclination towards each other; whether they are married, soulmates, dating, or are just at the early stages of their romantic relationship.

In essence, love may not be summarized with a few words because it is almost as mysterious as the universe itself. However, most people know and can quickly pinpoint the signs that follow "love" (in this case, romantic love).

What are the signs that accompany romantic love (being' in-love?')

When you're *'in-love,'* there are some classical signs that you will begin to exhibit. Here are a few of them:

1. **You idealize your partner**

When you begin to develop romantic feelings for someone, one of the first things you will notice is your tendency to idealize them. They become the perfect example of what a person should be. You see them as perfect, their flaws are lost in the vortex of admiration you have for them, and their character quirks are positively amplified before you.

If you do not pay extra attention, they may become the yardstick with which you measure everyone else in your life, and everyone who does not measure up may become less than acceptable to you.

2. **You make sacrifices for them**

One significant sign that you are in love with a person is that you do not mind making sacrifices for them. You derive some sort of joy in being there for them, even when it is not convenient for you. You want to be the one they always remember because you were there for them when they need it the most, and there is nothing too big for you to do or give up for them.

This is usually sponsored by the feelings of euphoria that surround your relationship with them. The same can and should also be said about them. If they are in love with you, they are also willing to make enormous sacrifices for you.

3. **You look forward to being with them**

You know those feelings of lonesomeness that accompany the exit of the person you love from your line of sight? That is one of the first things that happen when you are in love with someone. You want to be with them at all times. Their company is soothing to you and something you look forward to with all of your heart.

When you are not with them, you feel that gaping emptiness within you, and the knee-jerk reaction will be to reach out to them in some way; either by shooting them a text or by putting a call across for no reason.

In addition to this, you find out that you love talking to them. You don't mind putting a call across to them to talk about little nothings in your life. While you do this, you do not watch the clock as time passes. Time seems to standstill.

4. **You have great chemistry and a healthy sex life**

One of the signs that you are in love with someone is that they are super attractive. Most times, you feel the sparks that fly between you, and the attraction you feel for yourselves is palpable.

If you are to take this feeling to the room of your choice, the connection you feel with them and the attraction you share will spark things up to such a large extent. Sex does not have to be the focus of a romantic relationship, but when it is, it can help strengthen the relationship and make the parties closer to themselves.

5. **You feel a deep connection with them**

Being in love can make you feel a deep sense of connection with the other person. The deeper the feelings you have for them, the stronger this connection will be.

When you are with the person you love, you feel like you can be honest with them. You do not feel the excessive desire to impress them by putting up a facade.

A part of you knows that they can see the real you without judging or condemning you. At best, if they see a side of you that needs working on, they will help you straighten those parts out and play a massive role in your emancipation.

This connection is more profound if you are in a relationship with someone you believe is your soulmate. The depths of these kinds of relationships go beyond the physical attraction you feel for them.

It gets down to a place where the connection almost feels divine. You feel as though the universe holds you together, and there is some form of telepathy you share with your soulmate.

Being in love with another person is a positively intoxicating feeling. However, not experiencing love in a person's life can be ultimately destructive.

Here's why.

What happens when you do not experience love in your life?

This can be frightening!

The effects of not experiencing love in your life are numerous and primarily negative. Some of them are;

1. **Low self-esteem**

When you do not experience love in your life, you may battle with acute levels of low self-esteem. This is because the attention and care needed to convince your mind that you are worth something to the world around you are not in place.

As a result, you may interpret that lack of attention, love, and care as worthlessness. This, in turn, will reflect in every other aspect of your life as you grow and meet new people.

2. The tendency to self-destruct

In extreme cases, the low self-esteem you experience can deteriorate into self-destruction. Under these circumstances, you might be inclined toward harming yourself. You may even tell yourself that you're not needed in this world and that no one will miss you when you die.

Self-destruction can manifest itself in many ways, including suicide and suicidal thoughts. Self-sabotaging can also sink in when you consciously stop reaching for and achieving bigger goals in life. You might even develop a complacent attitude toward life, amongst other negative expressions.

3. Hurting other people

It's difficult (if not borderline impossible) for people to give what they did not experience. This is why it's common to see people mistreated by their parents and guardians as children growing up do the same thing to their children.

When a person lacks love and has never experienced it in their lives, there is every possibility that they will lash out toward others in their lives, resulting in the creation of a vicious cycle of bitterness and anger. With all these in mind, here's why finding love is essential on all levels.

Why romantic love is important

What's all the fuss about romantic love? Why do many write about it in books, and numerous filmmakers try to depict love in their movies? What makes "love" so strong that thousands of songs have been written and focused on this one subject?

Why do humans secretly crave romance so much? What makes love so important that everyone wants to experience it in some way in their lives? You might sweep your cravings for love under the carpet and behave as though you don't care about it, but you wake up each night with a thirst for it.

Let's try to answer these questions next.

1. Love plays a significant role in helping you develop a healthy sense of self-worth

Let's begin with the child who is yet tender.

When a child is born, the hope is that they are in a fully-functional family. A fully-functional family (in this context) consists of parents who love themselves and are not scared to show the love they have for that child.

Besides, these parents must love their children and teach their children to love and remain attentive and affectionate. This implies that the child is born into a family that prioritizes love and pays attention to all family members.

When the child grows under these conditions (with attentive parents and loving siblings), one of the things that will happen to him/her is that they will be surrounded by an empowering atmosphere. The words their parents say to them will be healthy and full of love.

These will be words that remind the child of how amazing they are and how they are loved.

The result of this is that the child steps into the world knowing that they are loved, cherished, and have the attention of the people in their family. This way, even if they have to face challenges in life, they can draw from the atmosphere and mindset their family has already created for them to keep low self-esteem away from their mental space.

This is the same thing that happens when a person is in a romantic relationship with a partner that loves, appreciates, celebrates, and constantly reminds them of how awesome they are. The attention they get from their partner becomes a springboard to help them skyrocket their sense of self-esteem.

When they constantly hear of how good they look or how awesome they are, this forms their mindset. When their minds are set on the fact that they are good enough in themselves, they can't suffer from low self-esteem.

If you are in a relationship with a partner who constantly feels self-conscious or a bit inadequate, make it a point of duty to remind them just how much they mean to you and of all the blessings they bring to your life. This way, you play a significant role in helping them build up their sense of self-esteem.

2. **Love can help you remain secure in the face of uncertain events of the future.**

One of the primary reasons people are afraid of what has not yet happened to them is that they do not know what it is, how it will come, and if they will withstand the pressures that come from the uncertain events in the future.

One sure way to withstand these pressures and the challenges that come with an uncertain future is to have a soulmate or a partner in your life. At least, you are assured that there is a constant in your life.

You can know that no matter how bleak the future may seem, there is one person who can and will hold your hands to give them the needed emotional, physical, mental, and psychological support they need.

You can count on your partner that you are in love with to come through for you, believe in you when other people do not, and stand-in for you when you desperately need help. This way, you can conquer whatever life throws at you.

It is easier to tread through your life's most uncertain times when you know that you have a partner who is in love with you and who you can trust with everything you have.

3. **Love breeds trust**

Everyone wants that person they can trust. That unicorn with whom they can be honest with without being afraid; someone who can know their deepest secrets and ugliest fears without judging or making them feel bad for being human.

The good news is that love can serve as a breeding ground for trust. This may not always be the case (meaning that both do not always go hand in glove), but it can often be the case.

When you are in a romantic relationship with someone, you will begin to notice many emotions flaring up inside you. Amongst these emotions will include affection, happiness when you are with them, and trust.

This is traceable to the amount of time you spend with them and the kinds of activities you participate in together.

If you spend time together embraced in intimate conversations, the trust will increase. Besides, if you can see through to their heart and their values are compatible with yours, this will further establish the bond of trust between you.

The result of this trust is that you will have a healthier relationship with them. Since there is nothing to hide, you can lean into the relationship without worrying if the other person will betray you or do something to destroy all you are trying to build with them.

4. **Love plays a significant part in self-discovery**

You may not know many things about yourself until you get into a relationship with a significant other. For example, the spontaneous reactions people in love have are reflections of who they are inside. This is because they do not get to think about these reactions. Instead, they rely solely on their subconscious to process and act out these impulses.

For example, someone who may have been viewed as cold will begin to show a different part of themselves when they have fallen in love. They may become attentive and highly attuned to who they are in a relationship with. They may look out for their partner at every point and make sure that their love interest is protected and always safe.

Under these conditions, the love they have for the other person has revealed that they may not be as unfeeling as you might have thought in the first place. The challenge may have been that they could not show emotion and concern until they found someone whose feelings for bringing out the love in their heart and soul.

In the same vein, romantic love has a way of shining a bright light on your inert traits. Under the bright beam of love, your preferences, likes and dislikes, values, tastes, codes of conduct, and definition of morality unveil.

5. Love compels you to get better

Have you seen someone you used to know a certain way suddenly begin to get better and make remarkable progress in their character? Then you dig in and discover that they fell in love, and their physical efforts to do more and become better for the person they fell for resulted in them becoming an overall better people?

This is one of the substantial benefits of romantic love in the lives of people.

When you are in love with someone, you become attuned to them. You avoid little things that you do that might set them off. You try to make an effort to change or at least be better for them.

This is one of the benefits of love because while you make an effort to improve yourself because of your partner, you cannot be a better version of yourself on your own.

Everyone around you will feel the impact of this positive change in your character. They will begin to react to you differently. You will notice the change in your immediate environment as the universe begins to respond more favorably toward you.

For example, if you were never interested in personal development, but you fell in love with someone who prioritizes it, you will take your personal development journey more seriously the more you interact with your partner.

As a result, everything around you will change for the better. Your competence will increase.

You will begin to feel more in charge of your life, and your ability to set and smash strategic goals will increase. Finally, you may even get positioned for bigger and better opportunities at work.

Meeting and falling in love with the right person can trigger a chain of activities that will turn your life around forever.

6. **Love energizes you**

There's a spring in your step and a knowing smile on your face when you are in love. This is traceable to the fact that you are in a relationship with someone who loves you, adores you, believes in you, and is vocal about the confidence they have in you.

The first point we established in this chapter is

that being in love has a way of increasing your sense of self-esteem. When you have a healthy sense of self-esteem, you can approach life from the point of positivity and the knowledge that things will work out for you.

Also, the knowledge that your partner is there for you strengthens you for anything life may bring your way. Also, love fills you with emotions and feelings that trigger the release of endorphins in your body.

These endorphins strengthen you, give you the energy and the psychological strength you need for the activities you must carry out. These hormones also help you maintain a clear head throughout your daily activities.

7. **Love kills fear**

You know the cliché saying that *"two heads are better than one,"* right? That is what happens when you're in love. When you were alone (with no significant other in your life), you had to deal with everything life threw your way by yourself.

At best, you had a few friends and relatives who would stick with you to help you through your trying times. However, none of them could match the presence of a partner or soulmate in your life.

All of this changes when you meet 'the one' and fall in love with them.

With this unicorn love in the picture, you can be bold and pursue the demons that may have haunted you in the past and defeat them. When you have someone you are in love with (and loves you in return), you can lean on them, which will supply a surge of strength that eliminates fear from your life.

With the power of love, you can chase your dreams and live your best life without fear.

8. **Love reduces your sense of entitlement and selfishness**

Everyone has a level of selfishness in them. This is the harsh truth that many people would instead brush under the carpet. The average person wants to be satisfied before they think of the next person.

They want to be sure that they're covered and that all of their needs to accomplish a task are ready before they inquire if the next person has what they need for their tasks.

This sense of selfishness differs according to people.

However, one of the first things that happen to you when you fall in love is that your sense of selfishness begins to reduce. In place of the "I" language, you find yourself speaking more of the "you" and "we" language.

You might have been someone who rarely thought of others, but now you pause and ask how your partner feels about your decisions. You seek counsel from your partner and consider the cost of your actions. This is one of the things that happens when people fall in love.

As is the case with most things that happen when a person is in love, the results of these changes in behavior will not only be seen and felt by a few people. Everyone within your sphere of influence will notice it and will begin to see you in a better light.

When you begin to consider the effects of your actions on people and look out for others with the same concern you do for yourself, it can be said that love has had a positive effect on you.

9. **The health benefits**

As absurd as this may sound, romantic love comes with health benefits; too many to be counted. For instance, being in a romantic relationship helps reduce anxiety which prolongs your life.

Soulmate-love boosts your self-esteem and gives you a release of feel-good hormones to help you stay energized and healthy. The happiness that comes from love keeps you healthy and strong.

Romantic love is the next-level love that

everyone wishes they could find and experience for a lifetime. When you find your soulmate, make it a point of duty to make them feel loved and cherished.

Make them know what they mean to you. The benefits of being in love with them have been outlined in earlier parts of this chapter, as this can help you unveil a much better version of yourself. No one can go wrong with "love."

See you in the next chapter of the *'Find Love or Die Trying'* series!

Leave a Review & Grab Your FREE Gift on the Next Page

What Did You Think of Chapter 0?

My small publishing business lives or dies from your reviews. Good reviews helps me live my dream, bad reviews, well, you know what happens.

Leave Your Review Here
https://loveblueprints.com/review-chapter0

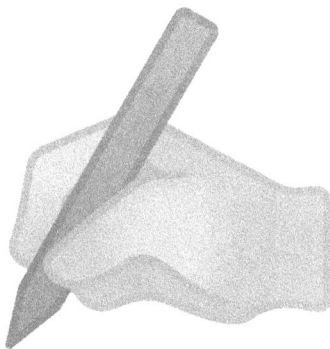

Tell my your honest thoughts about Chapter 0. It should take you no more than 60-seconds and I read all reviews and respond directly to you.

Leave Your Review Here
https://loveblueprints.com/review-chapter0

YOUR FREE GIFT

Finding Your Soulmate Tips Sheet

Sometimes you need a quick tip for a situation. This tips sheet points you to the best resources to help you fast! *(Get Yours Now...It's FREE)*

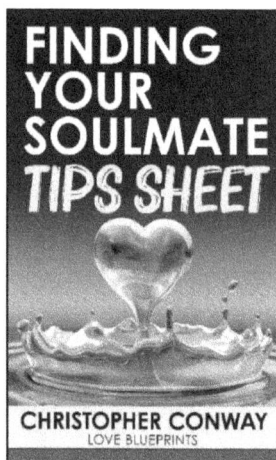

Request FREE Tips Sheet Today. Go to:
https://loveblueprints.com/fldt-tips-sheet/

Want to Get All Chapters in the *'Find Love or Die Trying'* Series?

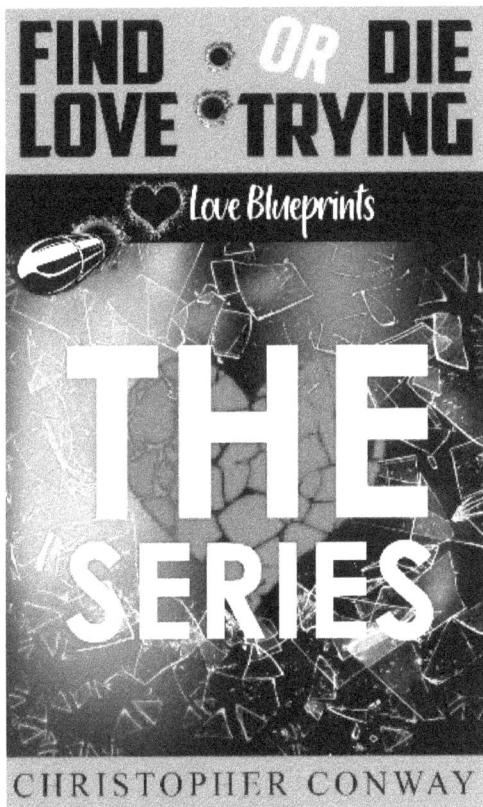

Go to this page:
https://loveblueprints.com/theseries

Reference List

Booth, H. (2019, May 20). *"Start low and go slow": how to talk to your partner about sex*. The Guardian. https://www.theguardian.com/lifeandstyle/2019/may/20/start-low-and-go-slow-how-to-talk-to-your-partner-about-sex

Center, R. T. (2019, August 11). *True Love vs. Infatuation*. Restorations Therapy Center. https://www.restorationstherapy.com/true-love-vs-infatuation/

Development, R. (2019, December 1). *Don't date girls who have lots of male friends*. Rebellious Development. https://rebelliousdevelopment.com/dont-date-girls-who-have-male-friends/

Donovan, L. (2014, February 20). *10 Places You Could Meet Your Future Soulmate*. HelloGiggles.

https://hellogiggles.com/lifestyle/10-places-meet-future-soulmate/

Fellizar, K. (2018, October 1). *7 Signs You're Not Actually Your Partner's Soulmate, You're Just Their Type*. Bustle. https://www.bustle.com/p/7-signs-youre-not-actually-your-partners-soulmate-youre-just-their-type-12108991

Gustafson, D. A. L. (2014, May 4). *8 Ways to Grow Love*. HuffPost. https://www.huffpost.com/entry/eight-ways-to-grow-love_b_4894123

Harra, C., & Harra, A. (2016, May 5). *7 Qualities To Seek In A Soulmate*. HuffPost. https://www.huffpost.com/entry/7-qualities-to-seek-in-a-_b_7201494

Kassel, G. (2020, January 24). *6 Reasons Why Sex Is Important in a Relationship*. Well+Good.

https://www.wellandgood.com/why-is-sex-important-relationship/

Kirschner, D. (2020, January 14). *When You Find Your Soulmate at the Wrong Time*. Love in 90 Days. https://lovein90days.com/when-you-find-your-soulmate-at-the-wrong-time/

Laderer, A. (2019, October 18). *How Your Partner's Past Might Impact Your Future*. Talkspace. https://www.talkspace.com/blog/partners-past-impact-your-future/

Laura, V. A. P. B. V. (2019, November 27). *5 Places Where you could Meet your Soulmate*. WordPress.Com. https://valentinalaura.com/2017/08/19/5-places-where-you-could-meet-your-soulmate/

Lawrence, S. (2019, June 10). *3 Signs That You Have Instant Chemistry Because You Loved Each Other In A Past Life*. YourTango. https://www.yourtango.com/experts/sarahlawrence/how-to-tell-if-you-have-found-love-with-your-soulmate-or-if-its-a-karmic-relationship-from-your-past-life

Leasca, S. (2020, August 24). *13 Best Online Dating Sites to Find love in 2020*. Glamour. https://www.glamour.com/story/best-online-dating-sites-to-find-love

Leonie, C. (2020, March 9). *Why Some Soulmate Relationships Don't Last*. Caren Reads. https://www.carenreads.com/question-of-the-week-why-some-soulmate-relationships-dont-last-forever/

M. (2020, September 19). *When You Meet Your Soulmate At The Wrong Time*. Thought Catalog. https://thoughtcatalog.com/marissa-hernandez/2015/02/when-you-meet-your-soulmate-at-the-wrong-time/

Mellardo, A. (2017, March 9). *How To Tell If He's Confident, Or Cocky*. Elite Daily.

https://www.elitedaily.com/dating/ways-tell-guy-dating-confident-cocky/1819258

Ohlin, B. (2020, November 7). *7 Ways to Improve Communication in Relationships*. PositivePsychology.Com. https://positivepsychology.com/communication-in-relationships/

Positivity, P. O. (2019, May 1). *How to Tell If Your Partner Is Your Soulmate (Or Not)*. Power of Positivity: Positive Thinking & Attitude. https://www.powerofpositivity.com/partner-doesnt-11-qualities-theyre-not-soulmate/

Pugachevsky, J. (2018, May 16). *7 Types Of Bad Men And Why You Keep Dating Them*. Cosmopolitan. https://www.cosmopolitan.com/sex-love/a20159874/how-to-stop-dating-bad-people/

Reid, S. (2016, October 14). *15 Reasons Why You Shouldn't Date A Mama's Boy*. TheTalko. https://www.thetalko.com/15-reasons-why-you-shouldnt-date-a-mamas-boy/

Santoro. (2013, June 30). *Are You Prepared for Love? 5 Ways to Prepare Yourself!* HuffPost. https://www.huffpost.com/entry/finding-love_b_3179023

Schreiber, K. (2016, January 14). *Yes, Being Vulnerable Is Terrifying—But Here's Why It's So Worth It*. Greatist. https://greatist.com/live/fear-of-vulnerability

T. (2018, April 15). *When Soulmates Meet At The Wrong Time - TheLoveWitchProject*. Medium. https://medium.com/@thelovewitchpro/when-soulmates-meet-at-the-wrong-time-2602cb8d19fc

Therapist, T. A. (2018, June 13). *Do you know your love language? (and why it's important)*.

Medium.
https://angrytherapist.medium.com/do-you-know-your-love-language-and-why-its-important-35c36ab986cc

Understanding Past Relationships. (2020, May 17). Therapy In Philadelphia. https://www.therapyinphiladelphia.com/tips/understanding-past-relationships

Weiss, J. (2017, January 21). *How to Use Your Intuition To Attract Your Soul Mate*. JIM WEISS. https://www.jimweiss.net/use-your-intuition-to-attract-your-soul-mate/

www.ingramcontent.com/pod-product-compliance
Lightning Source LLC
Chambersburg PA
CBHW032055040426

42335CB00037B/861